THE RUTH ANOINTING

Being Prepared and Positioned for God's Purpose in God's Timing

MONIQUE WHITE

Copyright © 2022 by Monique White

All rights reserved.

No part of this book may be reproduced, stored, or transmitted by any means - whether auditory, graphic, mechanical, or electronic - without written permission of both publisher and author, except in the case of brief excerpts used in critical articles and certain other noncommercial uses permitted by copyright law. Unauthorized reproduction of any part of this work is illegal and is punishable by law.

Unless otherwise noted, scripture quotations are taken from the Holy Bible, New Living Translation, copyright ©1996, 2004, 2015 by Tyndale House Foundation. Used by permission of Tyndale House Publishers, Carol Stream, Illinois 60188. All rights reserved. Printed and bound in the United States of America

Paperback ISBN: 979-8-218-18031-7

Book Design by Brand It Beautifully™ at
www.branditbeautifully.com

DEDICATION

This book is dedicated to every woman going through a Ruth transformation journey. May you receive courage, wisdom, and power.

CONTENTS

Acknowledgments	vii
It's Not What You Think	ix
The Visionary Author's Prayer	xv
MY RUTH STORY: BLESSING FROM BITTERNESS Monique White	1
Meet Monique White JD, BSN, CCRN, CPC	9
LEAVING FAMILIAR TO CLAIM UNFAMILIAR BLESSINGS Hazel Murphy	11
Meet Hazel Murphy	17

ACKNOWLEDGMENTS

Thank you to the contributing authors for bravely sharing the truth about your Ruth transformation journey.

To our family and friends who supported us during our Ruth journeys, thank you. Your support made a difference.

Special thanks to Allison Arnett for understanding the vision and the Brand It Beautifully™ team for all their hard work in bringing the vision to life.

IT'S NOT WHAT YOU THINK
FOREWORD

I can remember when I first read the book of Ruth. I was a new believer, and a seasoned woman of God told me that Ruth was a great book to read to keep myself encouraged and that God would always provide. As I began to read it, I was immediately intrigued by the women of the story – Ruth, Orpah, and their mother-in-law Naomi. I quickly realized that the book of Ruth was rich with insights! It is a healthy reminder to us that even in the darkest of times, never letting go of our faith remains to be essential to our walk as believers. Most of us know that holding on to our faith during a season of change can be challenging. However, Ruth's story paints a picture of a season of change and the courage to choose to embrace it.

Now, change is scary, but no matter how much our knees knock, change is inevitable. It is going to happen! Our God is a God of seasons, and each season is different than the other. There is one constant factor, change! Change is always present in every season. Some are meant for things to grow, and other seasons are meant for things to die off. Sometimes it will seem like your joyful mountaintop experiences with God last a lifetime, but then there are those seasons when the nighttime seems as if it will never end. I get it. I have had some seasons where during those long nights, I thought the tears would never stop flowing. You know, one of those times when we step into a season, and it seems as if everything is going to hell in a handbasket, you feel dry and empty, and despite your best efforts, you begin to believe you are a complete and total failure.

This had to be how Naomi felt. Naomi's sons died, leaving her daughters-in-law without husbandly support and no sons to care for her. This season of Naomi's life most likely felt unbearable. She must've felt so lost! In fact, the Bible tells us in Ruth 1:20 that when they do arrive safely in Bethlehem, Naomi tells her old friends, "Don't call me Naomi, call me Mara because the Almighty has made my life very bitter."

However, Ruth, in a difficult season, made a choice to embrace the change. This choice led her down an unknown road but ultimately revealed itself as her divine destiny! I believe Ruth decided she could no longer just follow God at a distance. She decided that Naomi's God would be her God, so when she was presented with the opportunity to go back to what was

IT'S NOT WHAT YOU THINK

familiar to her, she bravely chose not to. Rather than return to her father's home and stay in her own country, Ruth chose to accompany Naomi into an uncertain future in a strange land with unfamiliar customs. One day, we will all be confronted with the choice to accept change and embrace the unfamiliar as Ruth did. The question is – what will we choose?

You see, Ruth is a beautiful display of the kind of woman that allows God to mold, transition, and guide her through new seasons. Even if that new season seems to be a hard task, a woman that flows under a Ruth anointing will be full of commitment, determination, and resolution. It is the anointing to withstand and the anointing of service. Ruth's resolution to not desert Naomi positioned her for power, even if she did not know that at the time.

As a young girl, I looked forward to the summer season because I didn't like school. If it were up to me, it would be summer all year long! I just did not want to go to school. But of course, fall inevitably came, and school was back in session. You see, the season had to change, so I could learn new things, and learning new things would position me to be elevated. This is how God works as well. He teaches us fresh revelations through change. For Ruth, this season of transition and change was pivotal to her future. She found herself in a new position and a new place, all while learning how to follow a God that was new to her as well. However, Ruth did not quit! She humbled herself and allowed

Naomi to teach her how to navigate her new world. She learned new skills that positioned her for her destiny. Are you ready to learn?

Even though Ruth did not know what was ahead of her, what Ruth had going for her was her character. Because of the woman Ruth chose to become, she becomes actively usable by God. Her story emphasizes the anointing to understand and grasp the timing of opportunity. I believe God anointed Ruth with courage and granted her the capacity to enter new realms of His favor, and He is still anointing women of God with the courage to "glean" today!

Gleaning was a command by God for those with productive resources to leave something extra so that the poor, through their own labor, could provide for themselves. Gleaning the fields was hard work, yet Ruth set her mind to accomplishing the act. I believe God will fortify you with the courage and strength to "glean" during hard times. He will strengthen you to choose to believe!

Ruth could have returned with Orpah, but she decided to believe in God and commit. I challenge you while you are reading the stories of this book to commit to your season. You have been through too much to quit. Why endure all that you have endured just to give up now? Yes, it will require sacrifice, but you can do it! Your destiny calls and requires you to imagine your future. What will you regret 10 years from now that you didn't pursue? That you did not want to put in the hard work for? Will you wonder if you could have earned that degree, started that business, or be a true activist? Will you choose today to be brave and ask God to anoint you with strength, courage, and wisdom?

As a result of her bravery, Ruth ends up being in the lineage of Jesus because she became King David's great-grandmother! Imagine if Ruth had never left Moab and followed Naomi to Judah, David may never have been born! She is an example of a woman that when faced with hardship, recognizes that hardship is not hopelessness. She lost everything but gained so much when she focused on serving her mother-in-law. What could you birth if you would choose to focus and become loyal to serving the Kingdom of Heaven and the vision God has placed in your heart? I challenge you to dedicate your life to service as Ruth did. Servants finish their tasks, fulfill responsibilities, keep their promises, and complete their commitments. They don't leave jobs half undone, and they don't quit. Servants are great in the eyes of our Lord, and greatness is upon you!

There are many definitions for greatness, such as renown, grand, honorable, and important, all of which Ruth was not! She did not come from a rich family, she was not famous, and she did not have abundance, but she had a heart of service and love. As stated in 1 John 4:4, let us know that greatness lies inside each of us. I submit to you today that as you surrender to God, he will elevate you to a place of purpose that will blow your mind. Allow the chapters and testimonies written in this spirit-filled book to penetrate your entire spirit. Don't allow stinking thinking to rob you of the sweet life God has prepared for you. The season is not what you think. Ruth did not get what she expected. She gained much more. She could not have expected to become one of the wealthiest women of her time. She could not have expected God to place her in the King's bloodline! Your season is not what you think! Your season is one of provision, covenant, and increase! Although you may be gleaning, The Ruth Anointing of courage, determination, and focus is upon you! Continue serving, continue building, continue walking in love, and may our high God, Jehovah, who commands angels' armies, bless you exceedingly good! In Jesus' name, Amen!

With His love,

Dr. Maricia Sherman

Connect with Dr. Sherman
   Intimate Altar Ministries
   www.mariciasherman.com
   info@mariciasherman.com
   @mariciasherman

THE VISIONARY AUTHOR'S PRAYER

Lord, I thank You. Thank You, Father, for Your faithfulness. Thank You for being everything I need. Thank You for never leaving me nor forsaking me.

Thank You for the valleys as well as the hills. Thank You for every lesson taught during these times. Thank You for uncovering new strengths, talents, and knowledge. Continue to show me how You see me. Continue to use me for Your glory.

Lord, I pray for every woman who is going through or has gone through an analogous situation. Strengthen her, Father, according to Your Word. For You said that in our weakness, You are made strong. Perfect Your power in her.

THE VISIONARY AUTHOR'S PRAYER

Thank You for being her Helper. As she fights for what's right, remind her that if You be for her, no one shall be against her. Help her exercise patience during periods of disbelief and lean not unto her own understanding.

She shall not fear nor be dismayed, for You are with her. Contend with those who contend with her. Encamp Your ministering angels around her. Give her comfort and peace, knowing that You fight for her. Show her what You would have her learn during her season of testing and trial.

Thank You for working all things out for her good. Thank You for vesting her with power and authority to overcome all schemes of the enemy. Help her to walk in that power for Your purpose in her life.

Thank You for this opportunity to support and help Your daughters, Lord. Bless each author. Bless this work. I give You all glory, honor, and praise. In Jesus' name. Amen.

MY RUTH STORY: BLESSING FROM BITTERNESS

MONIQUE WHITE

Had the rug pulled out from under you? Lost everything? Were you betrayed, rejected, lied on, mistreated, or told that you were not good enough? Pain, failure, and embarrassment. We have all been through something at some time that could have taken us out – but God!

God turned it all around. God was present when everyone else left you. When others said no, God said yes. Can you relate? I can. Let me tell you about my Ruth story.

Everything was back on track. I had just reentered the workforce after a health crisis. I was regaining my footing. I opened my law practice and started serving clients. I picked up extra shifts at the hospital to stay current and compensate for any shortfall in funds.

Personally, I was happily single with no kids in tow because my son was off in the Navy. I could "adult" all the time! I danced a little jig in my living room because I couldn't wait to do everything I was unable to before.

I'd never been alone before. I went from my mom and dad's house as a student to single motherhood and primary caretaker. I was just learning and experiencing what my peers had done during their college years. You can say it was my version of the movie *How Stella Got Her Groove Back*.

I was never big on dating, though. It caused too much anxiety because I was a shy loner who always ended up in the friend zone. I was comfortable there. Those who know me might be surprised by this.

Why? I was into drama and music. Frequently, I was chosen for solos and starring roles. I was a member of a traveling choir. I was a cheerleader. One would think I was outgoing and an extrovert. Here's the thing. I could be someone else on stage. I was comfortable there. Confident in my talent. My discomfort was off-stage.

So, the Friends Zone hindered "Stella's" groove. Then a family member introduced me to his friend. I felt that if a family member introduced us, then he passed the test, he was vetted, and he was safe. I was wrong.

We pursued a long-distance relationship – talking on the phone and traveling back and forth to see each other. He introduced me to his family. He supported me during my mother's hospitalization. We both focused on our budding careers.

I didn't realize it at first. But slowly, red flags

popped up. Lies by omission. Misrepresentations. My calls were sent to voicemail. Plans abruptly changed or canceled. There was always an excuse. It all came to a head a year later.

I had my fill. When I compared the positives against the negatives, the negatives outnumbered the positives. It was time to end it, and I walked away. I deserved better.

But God has jokes. I'll never forget sitting down with a cup of hot chocolate and dinner. Immediately after the first sip, I became nauseous. Rolling my eyes and deeply sighing, I said, "God, really?" as I rushed to the bathroom.

A test the next day confirmed my suspicion. I was pregnant. Not exactly the best timing. I broke it off. I really didn't want to make that call. What would I say?

I finally gathered the courage to call. To say that the call didn't go well is an understatement. He didn't want another child. And lo and behold, he confessed to already having five! Five children with different mothers. Two clearly conceived during our time together.

I was shell-shocked. It punched me in the gut. I felt betrayed and played. After arguing, I slammed down the phone. I remember taking a shower and feeling so dirty. I sank to the floor. As the water flowed, I sat curled in on myself in the corner, crying.

After that, he told me that he didn't want anything to do with the baby. After he made sure that I was not recording the call, he told me not to call him anymore. He had political aspirations, and a child outside of marriage would derail his plans.

He went one step further and denied paternity and our relationship. He certified to the court that he did not know me. This kicked off years of court proceedings—endless contentious filings, endless hearings, endless fighting to defend against frivolous motions. Along with taking off work to attend hearings, he requested only for him to fail to appear. I was fighting to enforce orders for what was rightfully my daughter's – child support, insurance, and unpaid medical. I was fighting weaponized litigation.

In my mind, there is nothing worse for a woman than the man she trusted, cared for, and invested her time to turn around and deny ever knowing her when confronted. It is unfathomable to deny one's child. I could not wrap my mind around a person turning their back on their child for position and power.

All the while, I continued my law practice. It was doing reasonably well. I continued nursing, and I worked overtime to prepare for the times I needed to take off.

Then, my doctor put me on bed rest. "You can't keep working like this," he said. Everything that I worked for began slipping out of reach. All this while my daughter's father was out living his best life with no ramifications.

My daughter was born with medical issues, which

meant doctor's visits, X-rays, testing, procedures, and surgery. It was her and I against the world while still battling on her behalf.

I thought I was living in the twilight zone. Once the election cycle was on the horizon, I received texts, threats, and harassing calls from campaign managers Who does that? I didn't know where they got my phone number, but they needed to lose it and leave us alone. Frightened, I moved from place to place. Protecting my daughter was my priority.

One day after returning from court where he didn't show up again, he didn't comply with the previous court orders again, and the matter was postponed again, I was in my parents' bedroom venting to my mom.

My mom said, "Monique, the real tragedy will be if you lose your faith over this. Don't let this …"

I interrupted. "Mom, I don't want to hear all that right now. Sometimes people don't want to be preached to. I don't want to hear it because the reality of it is, I don't see God working."

I was going OFF!

I was not supposed to be here. Nursing school. Law school. Boards. The bar. I sacrificed so much. I had plans. This was not supposed to be my life.

I lost a piece of me during that time. I lost my confidence. I lost my self-value. My identity became what I had been through and was going through. I vented and complained so much to my family and friends that when they looked at me, they didn't see me, they saw what I was going through.

So, what turned it all around? I wish I could tell you that the situation had changed. It didn't. As a matter of fact, I am still dealing with it to this day. God didn't change the situation. He changed me.

One day I decided that I was not going to give it any more of my energy. Every minute, every penny spent on endless motions, hearings, and attorneys was a minute or penny taken from my daughter. Every bit of energy I devoted to the situation was energy taken from her. She deserved better.

If I said that I trusted God, then I needed to trust Him with all of it. I handed it over to Him. I refused to engage anymore. God entrusted me with this precious little life. It was my duty to give my all to her.

I later learned a different perspective. God removed someone from my life who could not go with me into my new season. I couldn't step into where God wanted me to go dragging baggage.

Frequently, I pray, "Lord, what am I to learn in this season or situation?" And because I sometimes miss things, I also pray, "Show me clearly so that there is no ambiguity."

Here is what I learned. In my bitterness, in my brokenness, God was up to something. In my embarrassment and shame, God kept me. When others whispered and left, God stayed. In my self-imposed isolation, God was by my side. In His faithfulness, He released me from shame, embarrassment, and humiliation.

If I am honest, what was meant to tear me down actually built me up. I used to hold things inside. I wouldn't speak up. I was more of a follower than a leader—a people pleaser. Someone frequently overlooked or discounted. Always on the outside looking in.

This experience taught me to stand up for myself and speak up. I found my voice. It showed me that I am stronger than I thought. I showed others that I am stronger than what they thought of me. It disclosed new insight and wisdom. It taught me to follow my instinct, to listen to that still small voice. It uncovered new talents, skills, and abilities. I'd been changed.

Too often in law and healthcare, we focus only on the issue we were hired to do. We lose sight of the fact that humans are multidimensional. Each dimension is interrelated with others. Legal issues impact mental health, emotional health, financial health, and relationships.

I'm not called, according to my experience. I am called according to His purpose. I have new insight and empathy for those in similar situations. I am more confident in myself. I have a renewed passion for helping those who others perceive as less than, weaker than, or more vulnerable. I'm a nurse attorney who recognizes that there is a whole person behind the issue.

That shy loner who preferred to be in the background is now a sought-out speaker confident in who she is. The follower is now a leader passionate to help women walk in their power and authority. The discounted is now regarded.

I've been prepared and positioned to help God's daughters in God's timing. Judge nothing before the appointed time.[1] All things work together for the good of those who love the Lord and are called according to His purpose.[2] Notice things is plural because it is the sum of our experiences working together for God's purpose.

Ruth lost her father-in-law, husband, and homeland. She lost it all and became a foreigner in an unknown land. Each viewed in isolation was terrible. In the big picture, God returned to her acceptance, favor, a husband, and a son—Obed. Obed, the father of Jesse. Jesse, the father of David. David, the father of Solomon. The progeny of Jesus.

Everyone goes through something at some time. It may not feel good at the time, but it is working with the other aspects of your life's journey for your good and God's purpose.

---

1. "So do not go on passing judgment before the appointed time ..." 1 Corinthians 4:5 AMP
2. "And we know that all things work together for good to them that love God, to them who are called according to his purpose." Romans 8:28

MEET MONIQUE WHITE JD, BSN, CCRN, CPC
BIOGRAPHY

Monique White is an attorney, registered nurse, certified professional coach, international speaker, Amazon bestselling author, and founder of Triumph Services LLC, a consulting and coaching firm. As a transformation strategist, Monique helps professionals monetize their expertise to transform their circumstances to live as God has promised-with love, joy, hope and power. It is her mission to break chains and transform lives.

A sought-after speaker, frequent podcast guest, and host of the shows Real Talk and Chrysalis Effect™, Monique has been described as visionary, anointed, driven, encouraging, and persistent. Whether she is speaking at a conference or workshop, being a panelist, consulting on business or legal matters, or just holding a patient's hand; Monique's passion for propelling and empowering others shines through. She is truly a leader who serves.

CONNECT WITH HER:

Website:
    www.triumphsvcs.com

Join her Communities:

    www.facebook.com/groups/womentranformed
    www.facebook.com/groups/transformedentrepreneur

facebook.com/triumphsvcs
instagram.com/triumphsvcs

LEAVING FAMILIAR TO CLAIM UNFAMILIAR BLESSINGS

HAZEL MURPHY

Be strong and of good courage; be not afraid, neither be thou dismayed: for the Lord thy God is with thee whithersoever thou goest. - Joshua 1:9

Life is a series of transitions. At conception, we transition from the spiritual realm to the physical realm of our mother's womb and tarry there awhile. At delivery, we transition from the coziness of our mother's womb to the many possibilities of this wide world. My mother was unaware until delivery, but I shared her womb with my twin sister. I was born the first of two twin girls to poor parents of a large family. My mother didn't have the chance to get prenatal care while carrying us. When she went into labor, we were born prematurely. And to her surprise, only minutes after I was born, at 1lb., came another little girl, bigger than the first at 3 lbs. Identical twins! Our airways and breathing were underdeveloped, and my twin sister, Helen, would not survive. I'm sure all routine measures of that time were taken to save my sister's life, but she passed away two or three days after birth. She had made her final transition, but my fight to develop continued. I had a pair of surgical scissors clamped in my chest to keep me propped up so my diaphragm could move up and down as I struggled to draw every breath. Months later, after I had reached 5 lbs, I was able to be taken home. But instead of going home with my parents and siblings, we paid a visit to my Grandmom's (my mom's mother's) job. That day, Grandmom was commissioned to take over my care. I felt isolated during those early years. Thankfully, even in this first transition, God had a plan for my life.

TRANSITION TWO: LIFE AT HOME

Most of my young years at Grandmom's were odd. Both of my grandmothers were older and lived very quiet, subdued lives. As a young child, I had no one to play with or talk to regularly. I missed the noise and comradery of other children. Although I saw my siblings in school and at church, I missed being in the house with them. Close but not close. Life was very different for me. I had strong feelings of loss and of feeling out of place. I felt like something was missing and like I did not belong. My parents, sisters, and brothers were poor and didn't always have enough to eat sometimes, but I wanted to live with them just the same. I missed my twin sister, who I'd never truly known, but I felt her absence just the same. I remember staring at her name on the "Lost Loved Ones" plaque in the vestibule at church and thinking, "why did she die, and I survive?"

Transition was a way of life for me. I mainly lived at Grandmom's, but sometimes I'd ping pong from there to my parent's house and back. At my parent's house, I had a different experience. Daddy and Mommy were not saved then, so they drank, smoked, and partied. Extended family, with all their kids and friends, would come and cram into our small house, and there would be music, playing cards, and gambling. Just a lot of hustle and bustle. The kids would all play made-up games, play tricks on each other, and compare city life to country life.

My childhood was a mostly happy one. Aside from feeling lonely because there were no other children living in the house with me, there were other things that made my home feel different.

I wasn't allowed to do some of the everyday things that a lot of the other neighborhood kids did. Before and after school consisted of feeding the many animals we had. After the chickens and ducks were fed, the hens were let out of the henhouse, and the eggs needed to be collected. Then I had to gather ashes from the coal-burning stove in the basement for soap making. Then it was on to feeding the dog and cats and watering the plants and garden.

Great Grandmom was a woman of God, full of faith, and a prayer warrior. I know that she and Grandmom loved me. I will always refer back to the days there. The noonday prayers, the weekend shut-ins at the church with me falling asleep on the small carpet square remnant we used to kneel on. I was in a God-fearing home – well cared for and prayed over.

TRANSITION THREE: CHURCH HOMES

I mostly enjoyed church. I accepted the Lord as a very young teen and at that time, I was the only saved teen at my church. So, again, I felt the feeling of loneliness. It was just me, surrounded by older people. Thank God, I still loved learning about God and who He was, singing in the choir learning about the Bible, and telling others that the Lord wanted to give them a new life!

As I grew older I began having dreams and visions that were scary to me. I would stand up at noonday prayer and share my fears, but I was always told to "just pray about it."

Eventually, I would leave the comfort of Grandmom's house for the last time and finally live with Mommy and Daddy! But that was short-lived. When I was 16, I moved to another home near my parents and remained there until I turned 18. At 18, I moved to Vineland, NJ. This time I, for sure, felt led by God to go there. So when the door opened, I walked through it. This led me to join a new church home and would lead to me hearing God in new ways and getting clear on my purpose.

The dreams and visions continued, and so did my search for revelations about "my why." It was then that I felt called into ministry. This left me feeling conflicted because, in my previous church home, this was unacceptable for a woman. Would I listen to the voices in my head saying don't do it, or would I answer the call? I dared to answer the call, accepted my place in ministry, and walked straight into what God had for me.

I started out moving from home to home then that changed to me moving from one church home to another. Each time I transitioned, it always seemed that God placed me in each specific place for a season and a reason. Looking back, I can see God's hand all over my life, leading and guiding me from place to place, from familiar to unfamiliar.

To follow the path God has for us, we must be willing to trust that He will guide and direct us. In Ruth's story, Moab represents the familiar we may be called to leave behind in order to embrace our Bethlehem, Boaz, and blessings – the unfamiliar. That familiar place held no more provision or promise for Ruth. She didn't know what she was walking toward but she chose to trust God and go anyway. Jeremiah 29:11 says, "For I know the plans I have for you, declares the Lord, plans to prosper you and not harm you, plans to give you hope and a future." Even when we feel afraid of change and afraid of the unfamiliar, we must follow the nudging of the Holy Spirit. He will never lead you from familiar to unfamiliar just to leave you. "Be strong and of a good courage; be not afraid, neither be thou dismayed: for the Lord thy God is with thee whithersoever thou goest." - Joshua 1:9

MEET HAZEL MURPHY
BIOGRAPHY

Hazel Murphy was brought up in a Pentecostal home. She attended Greater Mount Carmel Church in Berlin, NJ for the majority of her youth. As an young teen she accepted the Lord as her personal Savior. In the late 1970's, under the direction of Pastor Donald Mays, she accepted the call into the Ministry later relocating to North Carolina. Upon returning to New Jersey many years later, she returned to her calling in Ministry at

Emmanuel Temple Pentecostal Holiness Church, in Beverly, NJ, under direction of Bishop Elect Michael Young where she currently attends church. She has been married for 44 years, and is the mother of two adult children

www.ingramcontent.com/pod-product-compliance
Lightning Source LLC
Chambersburg PA
CBHW072025060426
42449CB00034B/2458